Seven CHOICES FOR SUCCESS AND SIGNIFICANCE

How to Live Life From The Inside Out

NIDO R. QUBEIN

"The power to **affect your future** lies within your own hands."

~ NIDO QUBEIN

simple truths®

Published by Simple Truths, LLC
1952 McDowell Road, Suite 300
Naperville, Illinois 60563
800-900-3427

Design: Rich Nickel
Photos: ThinkStock, Steve Terrill, Bruce Heinemann, Rich Nickel

Printed and bound in the United States of America

ISBN: 978-1-60810-150-4

03 WOZ 12

TABLE *of* CONTENTS

Seven Choices for
Success *and*
Significance

How to Live Life from the Inside Out

Regardless of where you were born or what your financial position in life, the power to affect your own future lies within your own hands. Where I am today—the President of High Point University, the Chairman of Great Harvest Bread Company and director of several New York Stock Exchange companies—as well as my experiences as an entrepreneur, consultant and author, are very different from where I started in life. Let me share with you my personal story and how the choices I made changed the direction of my life.

I came to America from the Middle East at age 17, with little knowledge of English, no money and no connections. While I arrived in America with little in my pocket, I came with abundance in my heart—including a belief that if you work hard enough and smart enough, you can make good things happen in your life.

"Each of us has the **freedom to choose** how we will respond to the circumstances in which we find ourselves."

~ Nido Qubein

So, I chose to build a life of success and significance, working my way first through a small school in North Carolina called Mt. Olive College and later through High

Point University and the University of North Carolina at Greensboro. After graduate school, I launched my first business with $500—a direct mail business, selling leadership materials.

This was in the days before the Internet so I would go to the telephone company, borrow the Yellow Pages for a particular city and work until 2 a.m., typing the names of churches or schools in that city. The next day, I would mail advertisements about our work to my mailing list and return the book to the phone company by 8 a.m. By working 17 hours a day, seven days a week, within four years, I had expanded my business to 68,000 customers in 32 countries.

Making that initial choice to work hard and launch my business opened doors that I could not have foreseen

> "The only thing that will stop you from fulfilling your dreams is you."
>
> ~ TOM BRADLEY

then. For example, I began receiving invitations to speak at churches and schools. By 1977, I was one of the busiest speakers in America, giving 200 speeches across the country every year.

From that first business, came a successful consulting business, and later the launch of the American Bank & Trust Company in 1985. I was the largest single shareholder in the bank, which was later acquired by BB&T, today a $175 billion bank with 30,000 employees. I still serve on the board of directors of BB&T as well as those of several other companies. I am also chairman of Great Harvest Bread Company, which today has 240 stores in 44 states around the nation.

In 2005, I chose to take

"The will to win, the desire to succeed, the urge to reach your full potential... these are the keys that will unlock the door to personal excellence."

~ CONFUCIUS

my life in yet another direction, one that has been one of my most fulfilling choices. Having been an alumnus of High Point University, I was a trustee who was elected as incoming chairman of the board. Instead, the board persuaded me to become president.

In taking on that role, I had a vision for what the school could become. In 2005, High Point had a huge inventory of deferred maintenance, only 375 freshmen, and a total population of 1,450 traditional undergraduates. In

"You are unique, and if that is not fulfilled, then something has been lost."
~ MARTHA GRAHAM

five short years, we've transformed the university—raising $170 million in gifts and investing half a billion dollars in academics, facilities, technology and land, on the way to a $2.1 billion goal. Enrollment has skyrocketed to 4,800 undergraduate and graduate students and the campus grew from 92 acres to 320 acres with 45 new buildings. We are now nationally recognized as an institution where every student receives an extraordinary education in an inspiring environment with caring people.

I've been a serial entrepreneur, business consultant, professional speaker, leadership author, and now a university president. I love what I do and I'm passionate about the possibilities. Regardless of the career path that I've chosen in life, I've followed the same fundamentals that I learned from my mother, who taught me to go beyond focusing on money … to experience joy and fulfillment not because I had accomplished something, but because I had ***become*** something … to give back to the world and to ***live life from the inside out.***

The Choices You Make Determine the Person You Become

My father died when I was six years of age. If I had the power to change one thing in my life, I would have much rather had a dad—to read me a book, sing me a song, throw me a ball, take me to the circus, or talk with me man-to-man. But, that was not my fate. I learned that out of adversity often emerges abundance.

What does that mean in life? It's a concept best illustrated by the koi fish...

If you put a koi fish in a fishbowl and give it food and water, it never grows to more than two inches in size. But, if you put it in a pond, it grows to a foot in size.

The koi fish grows proportionately to the environment in which it lives.

Think about it. When the koi fish is in the fishbowl, somebody is giving it food and water. It has no demands placed upon it. It has no adversity. It is in a comfort zone. It is content.

The moment you take the koi fish out of the fishbowl and put it in a pond, the water is deeper and colder. It takes more for the koi fish just to survive. By necessity, it has to grow bigger and stronger so it can deal with its environment.

That's my story also. When you come to this

"Character cannot be developed in ease and quiet. Only through experiences of trial and suffering can the soul be strengthened, vision cleared, ambition inspired and success achieved."

~ HELEN KELLER

The koi fish
grows proportionately
to the environment in
which it lives.

country with 50 dollars, don't know anyone and can hardly speak the language, you have no choice but to *grow proportionately to the challenges that lie ahead.*

My mother prepared me with the life lessons that I needed to not only meet, but to surpass those challenges. She raised my four siblings and I after my father died, instilling in us the values we needed for life. My mother only had a fourth-grade education, yet she had a post-graduate degree in a discipline I call common sense. Working as a seamstress day and night to feed and clothe the five of us, one of the life principles she taught us is:

"Adversity precedes growth."
~ ROSEMARIE ROSSETTI

It is not the circumstances in which you find yourself; it's the choices you make that define the person you become.

> "I have learned that success
> is to be measured
> not so much by the position
> that one has reached in life
> as by the
> ## obstacles which he
> ## has had to overcome
> while trying to succeed."
> ~Booker T. Washington

Allow me to share with you *Seven Choices for Success and Significance* you can make to help you *Live Life from the Inside Out:*

Choose
Transformational
Patterns

"In the long run, we shape our lives, and **we shape ourselves.** The process never ends until we die. And the choices we make are ultimately our own responsibility."

~ELEANOR ROOSEVELT

The bottom line is this: *What you choose is what you get.* Five years from today, you will be exactly the same person you are today except for the choices you make beginning right now.

You make a lot of choices every day—what to wear, what to have for breakfast, which route to drive to work, etc. Those are transactional choices.

But you can also choose at any point to transform your life. Those transformational choices are wise decisions that can change the direction of your life—putting your life on a path to success ... and more importantly ... significance.

The people who I admire most don't live their lives by a "to-do" list; they live their lives by a *"to-be"* list, for example: I want to be more generous, more patient, more learned, more reasoned.

"Choices are the hinges of destiny."
~Pythagoras

While you can check things quickly off a "to-do" list, it may be several months before you cross something off your "to-be" list. And here's the other side of the coin: You can't have a "to-be" list, without having a "stop doing" list. To become something, you must undo something ... acting on an item from your "stop doing" list.

Those who live by a "to-be" list have discovered wisdom ... an education that serves them well for life.

"It is our choices that show
what we truly are,
far more than our abilities."
~ JOANNE KATHLEEN ROWLING

"Life is change.
Growth is optional.
Choose wisely."

~KAREN KAISER CLARK

Choose
Energy
Management
over Time Management

"I recommend you take care
 of the minutes for the hours will
take care of themselves."
~ Lord Chesterfield

Are you obsessed with "managing your time"? Too many people get bogged down with this concept. The truth is that we all have the same 24 hours in a day. If you focus on time, you might be held back by transactional things.

I think in terms of energy.

Is this activity worthy of my energy?

Why is this shift in emphasis important? Because you could live to be 80, but you could lose your energy at 60. You have 24 hours, but if after five hours, you fizzle out, it doesn't matter if you have another 19 hours. The issue is not the amount of time you have; it's the amount of energy you have.

Because if you don't have the energy,

you can't execute.

We are all like batteries. Sooner or later, we will lose all our energy. That's why it's essential to place your energy in something worthwhile. How do you do that?

*Focus on activities that contribute
to the greatest value in your life and
do more of those.*

*Eliminate the activities that contribute
little or no value to your life –
it's a meaningless investment
of one's energy.*

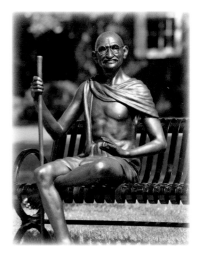

Here's an approach that works for me.
Regarding energy and time, I think in terms of
units—a unit equals five minutes. I never think of an
hour—an hour is 12 units.

To use 12 or more units, an activity has to be
something that's really worthy of my energy …
and that's determined by the results it leads to.

"There is more
to life than
**increasing
its speed.**"
~ MAHATMA GANDHI

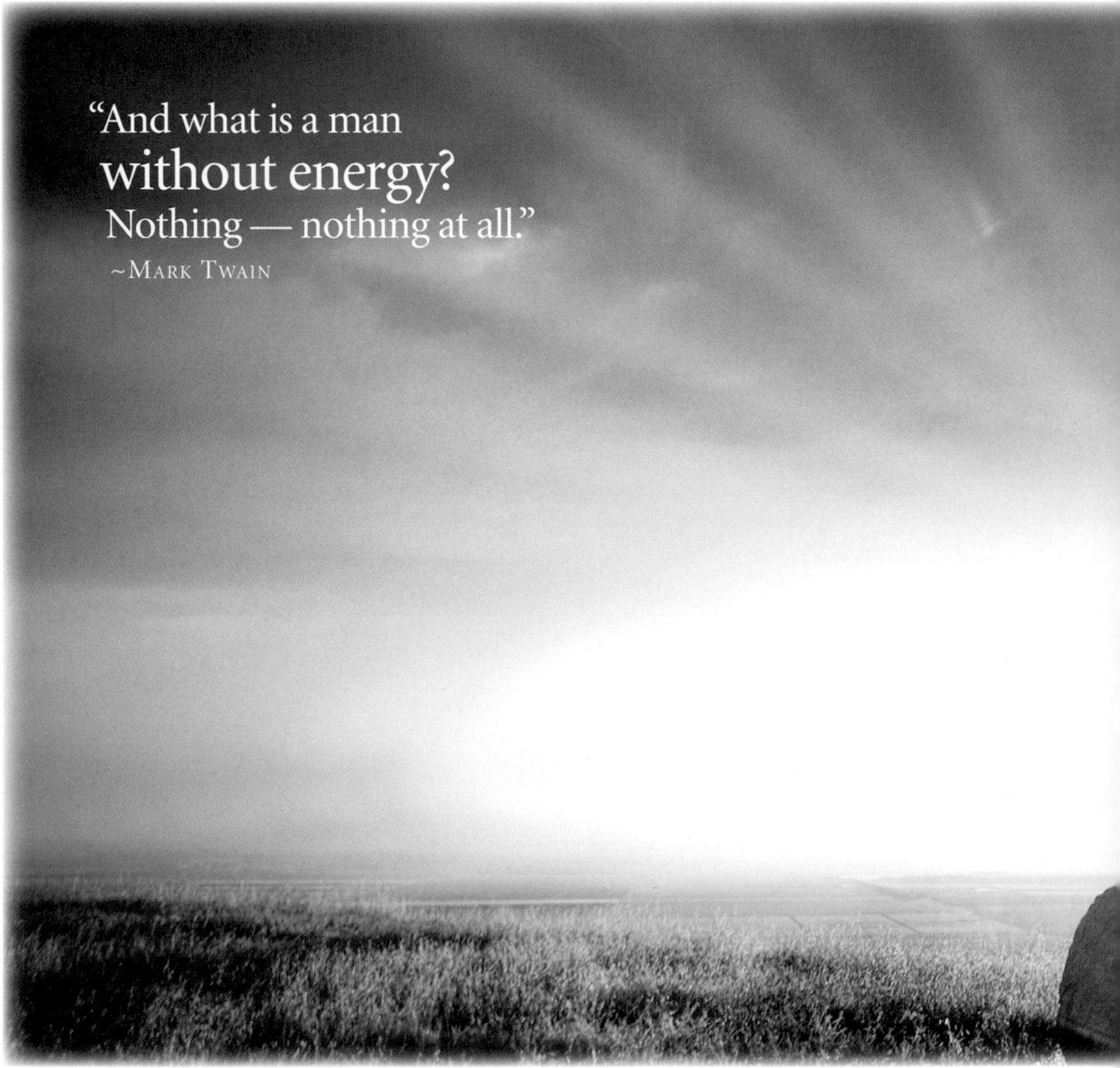

"And what is a man
without energy?
Nothing — nothing at all."
~Mark Twain

Here are a few energy management tips I teach in the Freshman Seminar at High Point University:

〜 Ask people who send you e-mails to limit them to six lines or less with ***one question per e-mail.*** I don't mind if people send me three e-mails back-to-back because I can answer them quickly with a "yes, no, or maybe." That's how I get through 300 e-mails a day and stay in touch with a lot of people.

〜 ***I conduct most of my meetings standing up*** and in the other person's office. That way I can leave when the mission is accomplished.

〜 My desk phone hasn't rung in 20 years—it rings in my assistant's office. ***I delegate and therefore, I don't get interrupted by phone calls.*** I rarely have more than a couple of calls a day to return … often from my car.

~ Keep time in meetings to a minimum—***Attend only meetings that are necessary.*** Insist on starting on time, getting and sticking to the point, limiting the agenda, and ending on time. Meetings can be big time wasters.

~ *Use every minute to pursue your goals*—For example, what do you do when you are caught in a traffic jam? Noel Coward didn't fuss and fume: He took out a piece of paper and wrote his popular song, "I'll See You Again." Many successful people keep self-help CDs handy to listen to while they are driving, selected reading materials available to use while waiting for someone, and routine paperwork handy—just to salvage time lost to delays.

Each of us is given 1,440 minutes each day,
168 hours each week, and 8,760 hours every year.
What you choose is what you get.
Take care of the most valuable resource—
not your time, but your energy.

"Real wealth is
ideas plus energy."

~Richard Buckminster Fuller

Choose to Give

"Always give
without remembering,
always receive
without forgetting."
~ WILLIAM BARCLAY

I believe in William Barclay's words. That's the way I live my life. I give of my time, of my money, of my energy, of my talent.

In doing so, I've discovered something phenomenal:

**The more you give, the more you get …
so long as you do not give so you will get.**

It's all about your spirit. I don't believe you should give until it hurts. *I believe you should give until it feels good.*

At High Point University, we model generosity for our students in many ways to demonstrate that a life of generous stewardship is more remarkable than one of self-absorption.

We live, they watch, they learn. We don't lecture about values, we model values.

"There is no happiness in having or in getting,
but only in giving."
~ HENRY DRUMMOND

Our students live in an ocean of generosity. And because they learn the value of generosity, they in turn, begin to give their time, talent, and other resources. In fact, HPU students give 50,000 volunteer hours each year and raise close to one-half million dollars annually to help those in need, both close to home and around the world.

It's all about giving versus giving back; loving versus loving back. It's unconditional. *Those who sow abundantly reap abundantly.* This is the way I choose to live my life: I invest one third in earning, one third in learning and one third in serving.

Many people looking for meaning in their lives find it by losing themselves in causes greater than they are.

"You give but little when you give of your possessions. It is when **you give of yourself** that you truly give."

~ KAHLIL GIBRAN

CHOICE NO. 4

Choose
to be Authentic

"The authentic self is the
soul made
visible."
~SARAH BAN BREATHNACH

Authenticity trumps charisma any day. People want to do business with people they like and people they trust. Trust is a big thing. If you don't trust someone, you're less likely to want to be in a partnership with them. Life is all about collaboration.

In life, you must become a "value interpreter" because in the absence of a value interpreter, everything is reduced to price.

Here's an example: If you go to buy a TV, do you know the differences among the various models? If a sales person can't "interpret the value" of the different models, you'll just look at the price. If the salesperson explains the "value" of certain features that are important to you, you might even buy a more expensive TV because it has the benefits you are willing to pay for.

"To be trusted
is a greater compliment
than being loved."
~ George MacDonald

The concept of being a "value interpreter" has applications in many areas of your life, not just in sales. If you want to apply for a different job, you have to know how to interpret your own value—how to sell yourself. And that's something that everyone needs to know … regardless of your chosen path in life.

If you want to have a great life, enough people must say that they need you in their lives.
Be authentic …
be someone other people trust …
and use the opportunity to interpret your own value.

"We are
 constantly invited
to be who
we are."

~ Henry David Thoreau

Choose
To Live a Life in Balance

"We come into this world head first
and go out feet first; in between, it is all
a matter of balance."

~ PAUL BOESE

W hen you are spiritually, physically, mentally, socially, economically, and intellectually in balance, you have the tiger by the tail. You have both success and significance; you have happiness and joy.

To reinforce this concept, at High Point University, I give all our staff and students an eagle whose beak is standing on an axis in perfect balance. Your life should look just like that.

I tell students … there is a time to be in the library and study. There's a time to sleep and rest. There's a time to throw the Frisbee, there's a time to go to a party. The challenge is knowing how to balance all of those.

As adults, we need to balance five kinds of capital:

∽ Financial ∽ Educational ∽ Reputational ∽ Relational ∽ Physical

Let's take a closer look at these:

∽ **FINANCIAL CAPITAL** is pretty simple—it's your money.

∽ **EDUCATIONAL CAPITAL** refers not only to your academic credentials, but to your appetite for lifelong learning.

∽ **REPUTATIONAL CAPITAL** is the reputation that precedes you. What good is it if you have all the money and education, but are known to be dishonest? It takes years to build this capital. Remember: "Your reputation is what other people think you are; your character is what God knows you are."

〜**RELATIONAL CAPITAL** refers to the relationships you create with others. Keep this one, simple fact in mind: *It costs you seven times as much to get a new client as it does to have an existing client. When you build relationships with people, think of lifetime value.*

Here's one example: If you owned an office supply store and someone came in and bought a $2 pen, you might think it's only a $2 order. But if that customer comes in every week for five years, that's $200. And when he comes back, he will most likely buy other items and he will also become your advocate—telling others about your great establishment. So never think of a customer interaction as a single exposure—think of each customer in terms of his or her lifetime value.

〜The final capital is **PHYSICAL CAPITAL** … your health. What good is it if you have everything but you are sick all the time? You are not in balance.

Now, we all know life is not perfect. Sometimes life throws you a blow—you or someone close to you is diagnosed with cancer, someone dies, or your business fails—if these things happen, you are out of balance.

That's when you need to have faith and courage. At High Point University, we didn't just have faith, we didn't just have courage, we had faithful courage to overcome obstacles and realize the vision we have for the school.

Sometimes, though, life is very tough on you. You get a divorce, your business fails *and* the economy goes into a recession. What happens then? You fall off the axis that kept you in balance.

> *At that point, you have a choice:*
> *you can be disappointed or discouraged.*
> *It's okay to be* DISAPPOINTED;
> *it's never okay to be* DISCOURAGED.

When you are discouraged, you stay down. When you are disappointed, you get yourself back up and slowly place yourself back on your axis. You dust yourself off and start again.

Living life in balance is a choice.
It applies to everything:

❧ Being **FISCALLY BALANCED**—you could spend your money and live life high on the hog, but then you might wake up in old age with no money. Instead you should be selectively extravagant and prudently frugal— methodically allocating your money appropriately—so much for savings, so much for retirement, so much for home, so much for fun, so much for tithing.

❧ Acquiring a **LEARNING MENTALITY**—What you read must be in balance so choose books and publications that expose you to a variety of viewpoints. Take a class on something you're interested in or make a commitment to enhance your career by enhancing your knowledge base. Read, listen, and observe everything you can.

~ **YOUR FRIENDS** must be in balance—Play golf one
day with one group of friends, enjoy a stimulating
intellectual discussion with another group or take
up a brand new interest with another group. Friends
with different interests provide a kaleidoscope of
serendipitous existence.

Keep your life in balance.
This anonymous piece of prose sums it up:

Allow time for work;
    it's the price of success.
Allow time for love;
    it's the sacrament of life.
Allow time for play;
    it's the secret of youth.
Allow time to read;
    it's the foundation of knowledge.

"Balance
activity with serenity,
wealth with simplicity,
persistence with innovation,
community with solitude,
familiarity with adventure,
constancy with change,
leading with following."

~ Jonathan Lockwood Huie

CHOICE NO. 6

Choose
To Be Positive

"A strong positive
mental attitude will
create more miracles
than any wonder drug."
~ PATRICIA NEAL

D o you know people who are cynics? The unfortunate thing is that if you don't **choose** to be a positive person, inadvertently, you may become a whiner. You whine about the weather and the economy, your spouse, your kids and in many cases you don't even realize you're a whiner.

But, here's the problem with whining:

Whining is the opposite of thanksgiving.

You are crying to the heavens that you are not grateful for the breath of life that you've been given. Defy that attitude. In fact, you want to be grateful for everything … your health, your voice, your work, your eyes, everything you may take for granted.

At High Point University, we give students a clicker that they can use when they hear another person whining in a meeting. When they hear the clicker in their own heads, rather than from someone else, they've arrived. They are policing themselves from sharing negative attitudes.

> "If you don't like something, change it. If you can't change it, **change your attitude.** Don't complain."
> ~ MAYA ANGELOU

Think about this contrast:

Fifty percent of America's households are ***almost*** one paycheck away from bankruptcy. Most of America's households have a net worth of approximately $100,000.

On the other hand, immigrants to America are not once, not twice, not thrice, but ***four*** times as likely to become millionaires as born Americans.

Why is that? They are thankful. They also believe that America is the land of opportunity, but they are thankful for the opportunity. They are not whining; they are grateful.

The first rule of developing a positive mental attitude is to ***act positively, and you will become positive!*** You can't ***think*** your way into acting positively, but you can ***act*** your way into thinking positively.

Deny yourself a "whining zone" and choose to be positive every day, starting from the moment you wake up.

"If you don't think
every day is a good day,
just try missing one."
~ CAVETT ROBERT

START THE DAY WITH A POSITIVE ATTITUDE

When you open your eyes in the morning, you set the tone for the day. Think of the words "alarm clock." Alarm has a negative connotation. What do you think of when you hear fire, theft, smoke or police alarms? So, why would you want to wake up in the morning to an "alarm clock"?

Change the name to an "opportunity" clock. It may seem like a small change, but when you wake up, you'll start your attitude off right by thinking, "what a great day!"

What happens instead is that some people love another five minutes in an unconscious state by hitting the snooze button. Then, they drag themselves to the window, open the drapes and say, "Good Lord, it's morning again."

Will that day be positive and filled with opportunities? With that attitude, one has already made a choice about what kind of day it will be. Why is all of this important to your success in life?

"A great attitude is not
the result of success;
success is the result
of a great attitude."

~ EARL NIGHTINGALE

*Your beliefs lead to your behaviors and
behaviors lead to results.
If you don't like the results, don't fuss about
your behaviors, examine and realign your beliefs.*

When my children were growing up, I would prepare an "object lesson" for the dinner table every night because I wanted to introduce them to positive concepts that are substantive. For example, I would tell them about what I was working on and extract a valuable lesson to remember. When my children grew older, they discovered that the cumulative effect of all those lessons evolved them into vertical and strategic thinkers.

Sooner or later, your mindset has a breakthrough…
I can, I will, I believe differently,
I'll do it differently.

Translate a positive attitude into action.
Execute on it in a measurable way. Whether you are an optimist or a pessimist, the choice as to how you will be in the future is yours, and yours alone. If you want to be joyful, enthusiastic, and excited about life, you can be, regardless of your circumstances.

"The choice as
to how you will
be in the future
**is yours and
yours alone.**"

~ NIDO QUBEIN

CHOICE NO. 7

Choose
to be a
Risk Taker

"The greatest risk in life is...
never taking one."
~ Unknown

The word risk has a negative connotation, but our country was built on risk. The process of growing and learning always involves risk and everything from the smallest entrepreneurial business to our country's space program was built on it.

I chose to be a risk taker. If you take risk out of life, you take opportunity out of life. The issue is not risk avoidance— that doesn't solve the problem— the issue is risk management.

"It's not because things are difficult that we dare not venture. It's because we **dare not venture** that they are difficult."

~ SENECA

Here's the **risk management tool** I use for every decision that has inherent risk. It's a formula of three questions:

1. **What's the *best thing* that can happen as the result of taking this risk?**

2. **What's the *most likely thing* to happen as the result of taking this risk?**

3. **What's the *worst thing* that can happen as a result of taking this risk?**

I make up my mind as follows:

〜 If the most likely thing to happen will get me closer to my goals **AND** if I'm willing to live with the worst thing that can happen, I march onwards.

〜 If the most likely thing to happen will not get me closer to my goals, it's futile for me to be discussing this risk. I move on.

〜 If I am not willing to deal with the worst thing that can happen, I must run away as fast as I can.

This tool is applicable to anything in life—from buying real estate, entering into a partnership, buying a business, evaluating a new job, or traveling to a new city.

If you use this tool, you'll make some good decisions.

Successful people don't avoid risks.

They learn to manage them.

They don't dive off cliffs into unexplored waters.

They learn how deep the water is, and make sure

there are no hidden obstacles.

Then they plunge in.

"Progress always involves risks.
You can't steal second base and keep your foot on first."

~ FREDERICK WILCOX

"Often the difference between
a successful person and a failure
is not one has better abilities or ideas,
but the courage
that one has to bet on one's ideas,
to take a calculated risk—and to act."

~ ANDRE MALRAUX

Choosing
Success *and*
Significance

"Success doesn't come to you;
you must go to it.
The trail is well-traveled and
well-marked. If you want to
walk it, you can."
~ NIDO QUBEIN

What is success? Only you can define it in your own life. In my life, I have attempted to define both Success and Significance.

To me, *Success is secular. Significance is spiritual.*

It doesn't matter how you define your own spirituality. Spiritual matters are always finer, deeper, and longer lasting than secular matters.

Success focuses on three Fs:

∿ Fans

∿ Fame

∿ Fortune

Success is focused on tasks, even goals.

Significance also focuses on three Fs:

∿ Faith

∿ Family

∿ Friends

But, *significance* focuses on *purpose*. Why am I here? What do I do with the talents, experiences and skills that I have? How can I make the world a better place? How do I plant seeds of greatness in the lives of those around me? How do I make an impact in the circles of influence where I find or place myself?

To choose success and significance, you must be a strategic thinker who:

~ Has a *clear vision* of what you want to accomplish

~ Develops a *solid strategy* that answers three questions:

- -Who or what are we today?
- -Who do we want to become?
- -How do we get there?

~ Employs *practical systems* to achieve your goals

~ Commits to *consistent execution* because in consistency, success emerges.

When implementing your strategic plan for success, it really comes down to three "Ds":

~ *Decide* what you want most to achieve

~ *Determine* the first step to getting what you want

~ *Do* the first thing that will start you moving toward your goal.

Using these seven keys, you can choose success and significance. But keep this in mind: success is not a matter of luck, not an accident of birth, not a reward for virtue. The most successful people I know are the ones who have something to do, somewhere to be and someone to love.

No one is responsible for your success or your joy. You must search for it and be in a continual state of earning it.

To merely succeed is not an end in itself. You must use your success to impact other people ... to impact the world ...

to Live Life from the Inside Out.

It all starts with the choices you make—they determine the person you will become.

"Your present circumstances don't determine where you can go; they merely determine **where you start.**"

~ NIDO QUBEIN

Dr. Nido Qubein came to the United States as a teenager, with little knowledge of English and only $50 in his pocket. His life has been an amazing success story. He has been the recipient of many honors including the Ellis Island Medal of Honor, Sales and Marketing International's Ambassador of Free Enterprise, the Horatio Alger Award for Distinguished Americans, and induction into the Global Society for Outstanding Business Leadership and the International Speakers Hall of Fame.

Dr. Qubein is president of High Point University, an extraordinary institution with 4,800 undergraduate and graduate students from 51 countries. HPU's intentional culture fosters the strategies outlined in this book. He has authored more than two dozen books and audio programs distributed worldwide in more than 20 languages. His foundation has granted more than 700 scholarships worth more than $6 million.

He serves on numerous corporate boards including BB&T, La-Z-Boy and DOTS. He is chairman of Great Harvest Bread Company with 240 stores in 44 states.

Toastmasters International named Dr. Qubein Top Business and Commerce Speaker and awarded him the Golden Gavel Medal. He is the founder of the prestigious National Speakers Association Foundation and speaks to business and professional groups nationally on leadership and transformational culture.

Contact Dr. Nido R. Qubein at nqubein@highpoint.edu For information on his speaking and learning resources: www.nidoqubein.com

"What if you could
be anything, or
anybody, you chose
to be? Think about it.
What would you
choose to be?"

~ NIDO QUBEIN

D r. Nido R. Qubein became the seventh president of High Point University in January 2005. Since that time, HPU has forged a new paradigm in higher education. Focusing on experiential education and holistic, values-based learning, graduates are truly prepared to live a life of both success and significance. The numbers tell the story:

	2005	2011	GROWTH
Freshman Class	375	1400	273%
Undergraduate Enrollment	1450	4103	183%
Full-time Faculty	108	259	140%
Campus Size (acres)	92	320	248%
Square Footage	800,000	2,558,000	220%
Buildings on Campus	22	83	277%
Parent Giving	$14,000	$3,000,000	21,329%
Employees	430	1023	138%
Economic Impact	$241,000,000	$442,300,000	84%
Operating Budget	$38,000,000	$154,000,000	305%
United Way Giving	$38,000	$150,000	295%
Study Abroad Programs	5	50	900%

Under Dr. Qubein's leadership, HPU has delivered on its simple, yet profound promise to students and their families:

At High Point University, every student receives an extraordinary education in an inspiring environment with caring people.[SM]

We invite you to visit and see for yourself this extraordinary place.

HIGH POINT UNIVERSITY

833 Montlieu Ave.
High Point, NC U.S.A 27262
highpoint.edu
800-345-6993

The
simple truths®
DIFFERENCE

I f you have enjoyed this book we invite you to check out our entire collection of gift books, with free inspirational movies, at **www.simpletruths.com**. You'll discover it's a great way to inspire friends and family, or to thank your best customers and employees.

For more information, please visit us at:
www.simpletruths.com
Or call us toll free …
800-900-3427